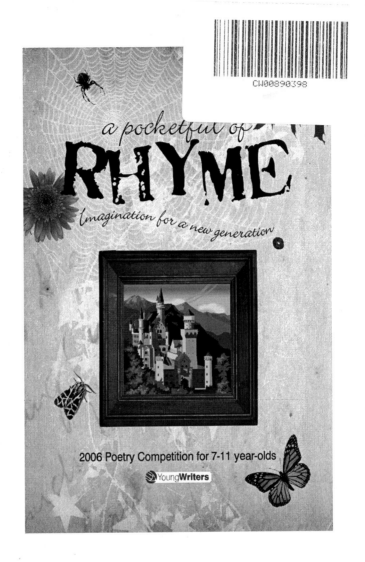

a pocketful of
RHYME
Imagination for a new generation

2006 Poetry Competition for 7-11 year-olds

YoungWriters

Middlesex Vol II
Edited by Mark Richardson

CW00890398

 Young**Writers**

First published in Great Britain in 2006 by:
Young Writers
Remus House
Coltsfoot Drive
Peterborough
PE2 9JX
Telephone: 01733 890066
Website: www.youngwriters.co.uk

All Rights Reserved

© *Copyright Contributors 2006*

SB ISBN 1 84602 470 6

Foreword

Young Writers was established in 1991 and has been passionately devoted to the promotion of reading and writing in children and young adults ever since. The quest continues today. Young Writers remains as committed to the nurturing of poetic and literary talent as ever.

This year's Young Writers competition has proven as vibrant and dynamic as ever and we are delighted to present a showcase of the best poetry from across the UK and in some cases overseas. Each poem has been selected from a wealth of *A Pocketful Of Rhyme* entries before ultimately being published in this, our fourteenth primary school poetry series.

Once again, we have been supremely impressed by the overall quality of the entries we have received. The imagination, energy and creativity which has gone into each young writer's entry made choosing the poems a challenging and often difficult but ultimately hugely rewarding task - the general high standard of the work submitted ensured this opportunity to bring their poetry to a larger appreciative audience.

We sincerely hope you are pleased with this final collection and that you will enjoy *A Pocketful Of Rhyme Middlesex Vol II* for many years to come.

Contents

Our Lady & St John's RC Primary School

SS Mary & Peter CE Primary School, Teddington

The Poems

The Deadly Cat

The tiger slowly glides
through the jungle,
with teeth like sharp swords
and eyes like luminous stars.
His fur is like a sheep
Beware of claws like razor blades.

Funke Olayinka (10)

Winter Poem

Winter,
Like a vice
Squeezing summer out of the earth.
Trees bent like bald old men
Chilblains
Nibbling at your toes.
Jack Frost creeps through the night
Freezing everything.
Snowflakes
Glimmering, as they fall from the sky
Blizzards firing icicles to wipe out the sun.
Snowballs,
Thrown like ice bombs
As snowmen stare with boredom.

Adam Kershaw (10)
Hampton Junior School, Hampton

Winter Poem

Jack Frost kills summer
Making winter
With his icy fingers.
He sprinkles snow
Making a soft white blanket.
Icicles
Hanging like a spiky curtain
Ready to drop.
Iced webs
Looking like shattered glass.
Leaves, sugar-coated with frost.

Harry Hornsey (10)
Hampton Junior School, Hampton

Owl

Owls
Known in cage,
Known in wild,
Either way, Nature's child.

As quiet as the prey itself.
Gliding through the night.
Catch the prey, grip it tight.

Eyes like pools of lava.
Dizzily flowing round in circles,
Holding the pupils hostage.

Wings are broad and wide,
But glides as silently
As an empty room.

Vinny Church (11)
Hampton Junior School, Hampton

Owl

It's dawn.
All creatures in the forest
Crawl into their homes.
Except owl creeping out in the night.
Owl glides smoothly
In the starlit sky,
Spreading fear over
The dark forest.
Eyes, like pools of lava
Searching hungrily for prey.

A mouse sneaking silently
In front of owl.
He has been seen, owl swoops down to grab its helpless prey.
Talons like two knives
Sinking into the mouse.

The sun is rising
Owl returns, satisfied
Until the night begins again.

Sasha Melkonova (11)
Hampton Junior School, Hampton

Owl

Owl
Has eyes as mystic as space
A beak as sharp as a butcher's hook
With dagger-like talons
Wings open in the night sky.

Owl
Brings death over the mountains
Carries terror through the forest
Ready to kill an innocent victim.

Owl
Sitting on a steady post
Eating its prey.

Robbie Lunniss & Pasha Beglar-Zadeh (10)
Hampton Junior School, Hampton

Night Bird

Owl
Intelligent, but shy,
Holds the midnight sky.
His colossal eyes tower over you.
His knife-like beak
Points down to his feet.
He glides,
Wings burst, in a symmetrical way,
When he spots his prey,
With his talons ready to grip and grab.

Owls
Feathers as black as night,
The time has come to start the fight!

Hannah Perrott & Laura Herbert (11)
Hampton Junior School, Hampton

One Of Wisdom

Fear over forest,
Smooth and swift,
Sweeps away the night sky,
And glides through the mist.

Wings unroll wide,
With a phantom face.
Claws like daggers,
Owl on the prowl.

Its lava pool eyes,
Stare through the coal black night,
Talons ready to seize,
With wisdom and pride.

Helen Thorogood (10)
Hampton Junior School, Hampton

Behind The Beauty

Owls
Golden wings,
So beautiful
Gliding gracefully through the night.
Its marble eyes so dark,
Full of sharpness.
Talons like blades,
Possessing its prey with terror.

Owls
Feathers full
Of beauty that hides its
Vicious streak.
The Grim Reaper
Haunts the minds of
Those who fear most.
Owl swoops down
To meet his prey . . .

Blaze Wallace (10)
Hampton Junior School, Hampton

Owl

Silent and swift,
The owl flies,
Flying lower,
A stealth bomber,
In disguise.

Its broad wings,
Fluttering lazily,
In the breeze,
Scanning the earth,
With lava-filled eyes.

Mouse and prey,
Remain silent,
For the Grim Reaper,
To arrive,
Waiting,
And waiting . . .

Suddenly,
A black tidal wave of fear,
Covers the forest,
Its fearful talons and beak,
Glistening menacingly,
In the moonlit sky.

It makes the catch,
Swooping swiftly,
Its sharp blades,
Sinking into the prey,
Morsel squeals,
In frightful pain,
There's nothing,
It can do now.

Annie Jones (11)
Hampton Junior School, Hampton

Fire, Fire

Fire, fire blaze and burn,
Make our cauldron spit and churn.

Deep inside the dragon's keep,
Take his scales whilst he sleeps.
Spider's leg and sting of bee,
Teeth of shark from mighty sea.
Beak of raven, grey wolf's claw,
Magic adds a little more.
Eye of bat and powerful broth,
Makes the cauldron choke and cough.

Fire, fire blaze and burn,
Make our cauldron spit and churn.

Anna Birdseye (10)
Hampton Junior School, Hampton

Owls

In the dark,
The dead of night,
The eerie hoot of the owl can be found.

Eyes like lava,
Red as blood,
His beady eyes,
Glance through,
The starry night sky.

His wings swoop across
The sky hunting around,
Starts to hover,
Snatches his prey,
From the ground
With his claws
Like daggers.

Amy O'Connell (11)
Hampton Junior School, Hampton

The Three Witches

(Based on 'Macbeth')

Double, double, toil and trouble,
Fire burn and cauldron bubble.

Dolphin's wing fin and owlets,
Wild bird's call and yellow wasp sing,
Howl of wolf and wild cat's cough,
With a stale smell of hell-broth.
Spiders' venom and wolf fang,
In the cauldron bubble and bang.
Snake slither and spiders crawl
Add a smelly rat, nice and small.

Double, double, toil and trouble,
Fire burn and cauldron bubble.

Shannon Painter (10)
Hampton Junior School, Hampton

The Bell's Gone, The Bell's Gone!

'The bell's gone, the bell's gone!'
'Right, be good, right be good!'
'The bell's gone, the bell's gone!'
'I hate school, I hate school.'
'The bell's gone, the bell's gone!'
'Do you think they'll be good?'
'The bell's gone, the bell's gone!'
'I'm not having anymore of this!'
'The bell's gone, the bell's gone!'
'I wonder if they've done their homework.'
'The bell's gone, the bell's gone!'
'I wonder what we're doing today.'
'The bell's gone, the bell's gone!'
'Right, assembly at twelve-fifteen, no, eight-thirty, doh!'
'The bell's gone, the bell's gone!'
'I hope they have remembered their homework.'

Peter Bell (9)
Hampton Junior School, Hampton

Where's The Bell Gone?

'Where's the bell gone, where's the bell gone?'
'Hurry up, hurry up.'
'Where's the bell gone, where's the bell gone?'
'They're going to be late, they're going to be late.'
'Where's the bell gone, where's the bell gone?'
'Have you got your homework, have you got your homework?'
'Where's the bell gone, where's the bell gone?'
'Why hasn't the bell gone off, why hasn't the bell gone off?'
'Where's the bell gone, where's the bell gone?'
'Yay, no school, no school!'
'Where's the bell gone, where's the bell gone?'
'Got to fix the bell, got to fix the bell.'
'Where's the bell gone, where's the bell gone?'
'Not organised, not organised.'
'Where's the bell gone, where's the bell gone?'
'It's packed, it's packed.'

Rosie Jarvis (9)
Hampton Junior School, Hampton

Autumn

Sad days of autumn when all the leaves
Fall off the trees and onto the ground
An autumn evening walking through the woods
Not a sound
Except for the rustling of the trees
As the wind blows between their leaves
It's so still and quiet here
Still untouched by human fear
The birds sing
The rabbits play
The foxes try to find their prey
It's Mother Nature's way of saying
'Please keep all the bad away.'

Lauren Caulfield (8)
Hampton Junior School, Hampton

A River's Journey

A mountain is like a child having a tantrum
And exploding with sharp, icy tears.
As it grows up, it is like a grandfather
With his icy, white hair and his long, snowy beard.
He is courageous, and has battled through many wars,
And all different types of weather.

The jungle is a huge green giant,
Which squashes you into its dark shadows.
You are a tiny ant,
Crawling through its green, dropping leaves.
Where streams of light peek through the rustling becalmed trees
Lots of creepy sounds surround you, rustling in the distance.

The ocean is like giant, charging horses battling the land.
It is also like an undiscovered black hole,
Sucking you up into its deep, salty, punishing waves.
The ocean is like swirls of colour dancing on the foamy water.

Chloe Fallows (11)
Hampton Junior School, Hampton

A River's Journey

The mountain is a courageous elder, watching over the Earth.
It has had many bruises and cuts,
Like a boxer punching its way through a mysterious life.
Although the mountain is old, it still has not retired,
Living on to its next life.

The jungle is a tall cavern covering the ground with its discarded leaves.
It is a tucked up world in the middle of nowhere,
With waterfalls crashing onto the rocks
Which fidget with laughter as they sink into the water.

The ocean is like an angry cat, opening its mouth to steal the land.
It is as rough as sandpaper
When it breaks its waves for another rebirth.
It can be as calm, as a mother rocking her baby to sleep
Or as fierce as a lion, chasing his dinner for the evening.

George Curtis (11)
Hampton Junior School, Hampton

A River's Journey

The mountain is a grandad smoking his pipe.
A playground for people who want a challenge.
They can be rounded or sharp, grey or white.
It is a pair of scissors, old and rusty, yet wise and young.

The jungle is a batch of clovers, a magical, dewy land.
The canopy of leaves is a tent,
Cutting you off from the world.
Chirrup, chirrup,
What was that?

The ocean is like a blue, green monster devouring the land.
The waves are as cross as a fiery dragon, being awoken suddenly.
When it is calm, it is like a dog lying happily by the fire,
Whining for the children to come and play.
It is like undiscovered treasure waiting to be found.

Cari Jones (11)
Hampton Junior School, Hampton

School Trip

'The bell's gone, the bell's gone
Let's run away, come on let's run away.'
'Look at them two, trying to run away, look at them two trying
to run away.'
'Just get on the bus, just get on the bus.'
'You can't get away from me, you can't get away from me.'
'That teacher's so spotty, that teacher's so spotty.'
'Get this day over and done with.'
'Bye dear, love you, bye dear, love you.'
'Very messy playground, very messy playground.'

Rosie Harris, Ashleigh Tull & Megan Dodsworth (8)
Hampton Junior School, Hampton

Friendship

A friendship that will never end
Might seem to break but only bend
And if you really are my friend
We'll stay together to the end.

When you're happy, I am too
And when you're glum, I am blue.
Let's keep our friendship honest and true
If you stick with me, I will stick with you.

Aurora Dove (9)
Hampton Junior School, Hampton

My Mum's Feet

My mum's feet are huge and they stink,
The smell reminds me of our kitchen sink!
They are big and puffy and particularly hairy,
My sister thinks they are quite scary!

Her toes are chunky and very, very long,
Quite frankly I think they were made wrong.

We went to the doctors about what to do,
Although when we got there, he ran to the loo,
He refused to come out until we had gone,
Obviously we weren't there very long.

Sometimes she asks me for a foot massage,
Although my dad pleaded with me to do it in the garage.

Once she wanted to go into foot modelling,
It turned out she looked like Shrek waddling.

Apart from the way they look, they take her where she wants to go
And I think that she owes it to her excessively big toes!

Aimee Spriggs (9)
Hampton Junior School, Hampton

Forest Essence

Forest essence
Full moon tonight
In the forest
Every corner
Darker than death.

Holding
My breath
In the heart
Of the forest
Dragonflies
Zooming around.

Mysterious
Murky
Is the forest
Dangerous
Atmosphere.

Taste of
Forest essence.

Rasna Jagdev (11)
Hampton Junior School, Hampton

Winter

Winter's icy talons grip the world
Turning it into a giant ice lolly.

Coming out if its ice palace
Waking from hibernation
Claiming power from autumn
Which is rightfully his.

Winter takes over
Making seeds burrow further underground
Hoping to escape its evil grip.

Until spring comes turning the world into a sunny and happy place.
Bitter with resentment winter crawls into its polar den
Waiting and waiting for his turn again.

Mollie Hughes (11)
Hampton Junior School, Hampton

The Jungle Band

I'm walking,
I hear quiet, quick, clapping hands.

I stop,
Vibrations like thousands of bands.

I sit,
Scaly rope tightens round my neck.

I stand,
Hear a sound like an old steam train
Something starts to . . . peck?

I run,
Vibrations on the ground,
Hear a big sound like thunder.

I sleep,
I'll never go there again.

Sara Deadman (11)
Hampton Junior School, Hampton

Angel

Angel.
Gentle amber moons
Blink, innocence.
Silky golden locks,
Curly as a coil of silk.
Butterfly wings,
Violet, scarlet,
Turquoise robes,
Ocean's calmest waters.
Voice as soothing as a nightingale
Enchanting as a hymn.

Gliding along rainbows,
Soaring within the clouds,
Sliding down sunbeams,
Climbing on air.

Megan Davis (11)
Hampton Junior School, Hampton

Planes

Plane flight,
Bird taking off, wings as propellers.
Hairdryers on arms.
Plane carers on board,
Friendly mums and dads
Keep us happy throughout the journey.

Plane seat, comfy beds,
Sheep wool softer than a feather.

Plane entertainment,
Watching the stars go by
Like shimmering musical notes.

Rhiannon Thomassen (11)
Hampton Junior School, Hampton

The Jungle

Parrots screeching as they fly,
Like darts through the sky.

Monkeys swinging to and fro,
Like acrobats, watch them go!

Orang-utans with lots of hair,
Watch them swing through the air.

Trees shooting up one by one,
Trying to be the first to reach the sun!

Tigers with their little cubs,
Are so cute I'd give them hugs!

Sarah Dennison & Gracie Jones (11)
Hampton Junior School, Hampton

This Witch Sarah Lea

(Inspired by 'Please Mrs Butler' by Allan Ahlberg)

'Please Mrs Hitler
This witch Sarah Lea
Keeps ripping up my paper, Miss
What next will it be?'

'Maybe her pencil case snapping my love,
Or maybe her breaking the dice,
Now go and get on with your work my lamb
'Cause that's not very nice.'

'Please Mrs Hitler
This witch Sarah Lea
Keeps dribbling on my scrapbook, Miss
What next will it be?'

'Oh, this is getting silly my dove
You used to be a dear!
Now there's one thing you can do for me
And that's *get out of here!*'

Kate Smith (9)
Hampton Junior School, Hampton

Dogs Are Fab

I like dogs and so do you
They are super and great . . . *yahoo!*
From Great Danes to Labradors, all happy and bright
They keep you happy all through the day and night!
I like dogs and so do you
They are super and great and I love them too.

Saskia Dyer (8) & Katie Page (9)
Hampton Junior School, Hampton

Christmas

Baubles sparkling bright
Like in the fairy lights
Having fun till the day is done, at Christmas time.

People shopping
Never stopping
Shop non-stop.

It never lasts
It's gone fast
It's a short Christmas.

Zoë Dennison (8)
Hampton Junior School, Hampton

Things Are Too Good To Be Bad

Things are too good to be bad
Smashing a window
Breaking a rule
Why does it mostly happen at school?

Things are too bad to be good
Concentrating in class
Not being a fool
Why does it mostly happen at school?

Things are too bad to be good
Bedtime at eight
Brothers having a moan
Why does it mostly happen at home?

Things are too good to be bad
Chicken goujons for tea
Calling a friend on the phone
Why does it mostly happen at home?

Ruby Hornsey (9)
Hampton Junior School, Hampton

A Christmas Eve

Look at the Christmas tree as green as grass
The presents underneath the tree shimmering like Mars
Santa in the night sky delivering presents all around
The star on top sparkling like the snow that belongs on the ground.

Carys Turner (8)
Hampton Junior School, Hampton

Water Can Be Used For Everything

Water can be used for everything
Drinking it
You can even play with it
We use it every day
Even when we play
We use it to clean things
Infact we use it for everything.

Akash Pathak (10)
Hampton Junior School, Hampton

Water, Water Everywhere

Water, water everywhere,
In poor countries it's unfair,
One person dies every fifteen seconds,
I hope those selfish people learn a lesson,
Dirty water's very bad,
Those people that have none are very sad,
And also very mad.
If they get some they'll be glad!

Lucy Voller (9)
Hampton Junior School, Hampton

Water

Water, water everywhere
It's everywhere you can stare
Up the drainpipes and in the air
It makes clouds that give you rain
Sometimes it can take away your pain
You can drink it
And you can think it
It fills up swimming pools
And it keeps you alive
It helps you to survive
Seventy percent of your brain is water
If no water, worldwide slaughter.

Adam Lovitt (9)
Hampton Junior School, Hampton

Water

Give a quarter and drink water
If you drink it you'll feel better
Drink water and live!
People need it, so give!
Water is fun to drink
Water is fun to drink.

Shaitya Setia (9)
Hampton Junior School, Hampton

Water

Water, water everywhere
Here, there everywhere!
Over there the sea's so big
Up there a little spring.
The water comes from a spring in the mountains
And ends up in your garden fountains!
First water is dissolved in the filter beds
Passed through the sieves and pumped to your home.
After you've drunk it and poured it away
It goes on its way to the clouds.
There it turns into rain and pours down into your drain!
So drink some water, you know you ought to!

Louis Jones (10)
Hampton Junior School, Hampton

Water

Water is fun
And cool in the sun.
Water is a liquid
With a load of uses.
Water is in a swimming pool.
Water is so cool.

Charlie Curant (9)
Hampton Junior School, Hampton

Water

Water keeps us alive
All of the time.
Time and time again there is water.
Everyone loves to drink water.
Water goes to places to get clean enough to drink.

Abigail Nichols (10)
Hampton Junior School, Hampton

Water

Water in the sea, water in the air
Water, water everywhere!
Some people in Africa don't have pills to make them completely better.
They don't have time to play, this time today
Just because they have to fetch water every day!

Hannah Chan (9)
Hampton Junior School, Hampton

Water Saves Us

Water is the thing that saves us,
We cannot lose it,
We shouldn't need to walk a long way for it,
We cannot forget it,
Water is calm and gentle and crystal clear!

Emma Bevan (10)
Hampton Junior School, Hampton

Water Clean Water

Water, clean water keep us alive
All around me, there is water.
Tell people we need clean water.
Everyone needs water like
Rivers flowing to the sea.

Senol Kasim (9)
Hampton Junior School, Hampton

Water, Water

Water, water everywhere
In the skies in the air.
Splish, splosh, splash, splosh.
We always use it when we wash
Water fights kids do it all the time.
Splash, splosh, splish.
Water, water everywhere.
Flowing through the rivers into the lakes.
Water saves lives all the time.
We use it in our daily life.
Crystal clear droplets.
Sparkles and shine
Water is good for us.
We drink it all the time.

Tayo Andoh (9)
Hampton Junior School, Hampton

Water

Water, the saviour of the world.
Water, the strongest force in the galaxy!
It keeps us strong and healthy.
It keeps us alive as well.
Water, the saviour of the world.

Jack Farrar (9)
Hampton Junior School, Hampton

Water

Water is the liquid of health
It improves your body and of course yourself.
Water can save you and your friends too
It all comes out when you flush the loo.
Water gives you energy and speed
It gives you the knowledge to make you read.

Laurence Kravetz (9)
Hampton Junior School, Hampton

Under My Bed

You can't see me under my bed.
My bed is mysterious and wild.
There are no brothers, sisters, demons or monsters in my room.
Also, there are chocolate streams and fountains.
You can touch the moon on my bed.
All of a sudden a knock on the door,
Then the secret place turns invisible.
But the best thing is no one knows where my secret place is.

Austin Streeter (9)
Hampton Junior School, Hampton

My Special Place

You can't see my special place
My place is nowhere to see
There are no evil people but a rich money tree.
Also there are people who like to play all day,
You can even see a river where you can relax and lay.
All of a sudden the lights go out
But the best thing is no one knows I'm here.

Andrew Tolfree (10)
Hampton Junior School, Hampton

Water Life

Streams come down mountains,
Into rivers and lakes,
Pure clean water,
Under the stars it shines,
It's our life, it's precious.
It's three quarters of our world
Hear the lap of the sea hit the sand.
Rain falls down into the soil,
Sucks it up all day,
It's our life.
We drink and use it every day,
You can't live without it.

Charlie Black (9)
Hampton Junior School, Hampton

Giraffe

Giraffes are tall with very long necks.
Their skin has diamonds just like little orange tiles.
Their legs are like long cocktail sticks
But they can bend their lovely long necks to reach the trees.
Their fluffy hair is as soft as silk.

Isabel Humphrey (9)
Hampton Junior School, Hampton

The Beach

White sand, turquoise sea,
Here we come my brother and me.
Off to have lots of fun
Splashing and dashing in the sun.
White sand, turquoise sea,
I dig up the sand to cover my knee.
Listen to the sound of the waves,
Find and explore dark, creepy caves.
The water is as clear as glass,
Bump into Tom from my new class.
White sand, turquoise sea,
This is the place for me!

Samuel Kintoff (10)
Hampton Junior School, Hampton

My School

You can't see my school
My school is on Mars
There is no evil and no monsters
Also there are gold walls, silk and chandeliers.
You can even see the world from here,
All of a sudden it booms into Earth when it's home time.
But the best thing it's my little school.

Lucy Hall (9)
Hampton Junior School, Hampton

My Dog Gus

My dog Gus is soppy, playful and cuddly.
He always wags his tail when we come through the door.
Gus is like a streak of lightning when he runs.
He flies across the fields like a greyhound.

Gus's fur is so soft you could lie on it.
Gus makes me feel happy when I'm sad.
When we go on holiday,
It's not the same without Gus.

When Gus sees a cat or a squirrel he gets very excited
And bounces like a bunny through the long grass.
Gus is happy, fun and exciting to be with,
I love my dog Gus.

Matthew Reed-Oliver (10)
Hampton Junior School, Hampton

Water Pollution

I've been here since the dawn of time.
I have been poisoned and cleaned.
I have been drank and spat out of mouths.

Now I'm slowly fading because I am being mistreated.
Humans have been throwing junk into me.
I can repay you when all you have to do is keep me clean!

Henry Beal (9)
Hampton Junior School, Hampton

Tammy

Tammy's the best and lover of all,
As cute as can be and so beautiful.

Running in her ball, up and down,
Speeding so rapidly, round and round.

She loves to climb all over the place,
Over my body and up to my face!

She loves her food, especially her nuts,
And greedily wedges in her fruit and peanuts.

She makes me feel as happy as can be,
I love to care for my dearest, Tammy.

Leah Atkinson (10)
Hampton Junior School, Hampton

Magical Tears

Water streams down my face,
Running through rivers like a race.
But the sad thing that I cannot bare is pollution, poison in the air.
Falls into rivers, streams and seas,
But if they've been drunk may cause a disease.

So help them, help them keep them safe
Then you'll have magic tears.

Magic tears are special,
Magic tears are bright,
Magic tears are happy and fill you up with light.

Harriet Frise (9)
Hampton Junior School, Hampton

Water

Water, water, how could we live without water?
Drink as lot as much as a pot full.
Water flowing and really growing,
The water glittered, glistened and gleamed.
But people retch, puke, vomit and belch
In rivers, streams, lakes and seas.

Alex Wong (9)
Hampton Junior School, Hampton

Days At School

Ring, ring, ring, the bell's gone, the day's just begun.
They're all lining up in single file,
Class 1, 2, 3, 4, 5, 6,
Mrs Turner is reading out the register, they have a full class.
It's literacy! It's literacy!
Jimmy's in trouble! Jimmy's in trouble!
Ring, ring, ring, the bell's gone, the day's just begun.
It's playtime! It's playtime!
The trim trail is crowded.
It's numeracy! It's numeracy!
It's lunchtime! It's lunchtime!
Kick a ball about.
It's Romans work. It's Romans work.
It's three-fifteen. It's three-fifteen,
It's time to go! It's time to go!

Tom Wingham & Harry Chapman (9)
Hampton Junior School, Hampton

A Surprise Christmas Visitor

A pointed orange nose
And black beady eyes,
I look into your window
And watch you eat mince pies!

A woolly scarf
And black top hat,
I don't want to be knocked over,
So keep me away from the cat!

My chubby white body
Stands out in the cold,
When the warm sun comes out
My news will be old.

Stony black buttons
All down my front,
For children to find me
They're really have to hunt!

Twiggy stick arms
Long and thin,
Children come up to me
To sing me a hymn.

Roll me around in the snow
And I'll be fat,
Decorate me with shiny stones
And Dad's cowboy hat!

I've told you about
Have you guessed who I am?
Yes, that's right,
I'm a snowman!

Kate Harris & Anna Gilroy (9)
Hampton Junior School, Hampton

Water, Water Everywhere

Water, water everywhere
In the drainpipes, in the air,
Water surrounds us in the sea
Water is good for me.

Dominic Cundle (10)
Hampton Junior School, Hampton

The Jaguar

Jaguar
Swift lightning
Knives puncture prey
Green emeralds gaze
Soggy sponge sniffs
Jungle trembles
Creature jet-black emerges
Animals flee.

Harry Fraser-Smith (11)
Hampton Junior School, Hampton

Down In The Jungle

Down in the jungle
Where the lion sleeps
I could see a gorilla
Smiling at me.
I saw a snake
Slithering up a tree.
I saw a bee
Flying past me.
I saw a parrot
On a thick branch
And suddenly it spoke to me.

Elliott Crane (11)
Hampton Junior School, Hampton

My Favourite Things

I like Ferraris, Lamborghinis, nearly all types of cars,
But I'd really like one that could take me to Mars.
I don't think I'd like a second-hand hummer,
Especially not if it was owned by a plumber.
I really would like a blue Mercedes-Benz,
It surely would set all kinds of new trends.
My dream car for sure is a Lamborghini,
I'd make it my wish if I ever met a genie.
Cars are some of my favourite things
But my sister would prefer diamond rings.

I like animals that live in the wild,
I've liked them since I was a very little child.
If I had a pet I'd want a big scary dog,
To frighten away the strangers when I go for my jog.
Tigers are the biggest type of wildcat,
They run after their prey so they never get fat.
If I could be an animal I'd be a grizzly bear,
I'd live in Canada, hunt fish and enjoy the fresh mountain air.
Animals are some of my favourite things
But my sister would prefer diamond rings.

I enjoy playing football three times a week,
The crowd cheer so much afterwards they can't speak.
I play table tennis at home with my dad,
He nearly always beats me and I get extremely sad.
On Sundays I play a nice game of cricket,
When bowling I nearly always break the wicket.
I've tried it but I don't really like hockey,
And when I'm grown, I will be too big to be a jockey.
Sports are some of my favourite things
But my sister would prefer diamond rings.

Amar Bhogal (10)
North Primary School, Southall

Puppy

I'm a puppy that sits and waits in the corner shop down Draton Lane.
I wait for my owner to come to collect me, I wait and wait.
I'm a puppy that wants to be full of fun,
Play and chasing, and not being picked on.

I'm a puppy, my name is Poppy.
Who could not choose me, I'm like a ruby.

I'm a puppy, whose dream came true,
I've been picked by an owner whose name is Andrew.
He's a nice man who has three children
And shall I tell you the best bit
I'm not a puppy who sits in the corner shop
But I'm full of love and not being picked on.

Harpreet Karwal (10)
North Primary School, Southall

Cricket Season

Australia vs England, it's going to be a good match
Andrew Flintoff is to catch,
England win the toss and choose to bat
And they go off to their equipment from the mat.

Brett Lee starts to bowl and it is an out
Everyone sees it and gives a large shout!
Ashley Giles hits a six and celebrates
But pretends to faint but he only fakes.

The score three-nil and it's looking bad
But guess who cheers, only his dad.
Flintoff begins to run but picks up a sprain
And definitely feels the pain.
Shane Warne does a spinner
He ends up a true winner.
England are losing,
That was not confusing.
Australia are batting now
They hit a large six and that was *wow!*
They are almost winning but they need a few runs
They stop for lunch to eat sausage buns.

Now lunch is over
England need a four-leaf clover.
The bowler runs up
He sees them holding the cup.

It's the end of the game
Australia's fame came,
They hold the cup high in the sky
And wave goodbye.

They're on their way back home
All covered in champagne foam.

Adam Shah (11)
North Primary School, Southall

I Once Had . . .

I once had a teacher
Who showed off her best feature
And loved every creature.

I once had a pet
Who was found in a net
And died from a threat.

There was an old person of Tring
Who when someone asked her to sing
She got told off by the king.

A little saint best fits a little shrine
A little prop best fits a little vine
It's all as easy as drinking wine.

I once saw some bread
Which was as big as a head
That we ate in the shed.

I was on a boat
Fell down and started to float
And then I wrote a little note.

I dug up some soil
And ate eggs that I had to boil
And made chips in the oil.

My brother has a fat belly
That's filled with jelly
Which he eats in front of the telly.

Aaliyah Hussain (10)
North Primary School, Southall

My Pets Are Totally Wrong

I have a cat that did a bark
So now I take it to the park
I know it sounds silly
But my little cat called Milly
Thinks she is a hound
Born with many others in a pound.

I have a bird that roared
So now I tame it with a sword
I know it sounds dumb
But my little bird, who for two chicks, is a mum
Thinks she is a lioness
Pushing away every plate of cress.

I have a snake that snapped
Who like a mummy, got wrapped
I know it sounds weird
But my snake, who by my sister is feared
Thinks he is a crocodile
And went to the canal to swim a mile.

I have a rabbit who bubbled
Even though she should have snuffled
I know it sounds crazy
But my rabbit's called Maisie
Thinks she is a fish
And wants it so hard, it's a wish.

I have a hamster that did a loud trumpet
And took a large bite out of my crumpet!
I know it sounds absurd
But she really tires to be heard
She thinks she is an elephant
And now, unlike she used to be, isn't at all elegant.

Gagandeep Jhuti (11)
North Primary School, Southall

Winter

Peering through the window I see
Snowflakes falling on me.

It quickly gathers like a white sheet
Around me and my friend's feet.

Rabbits running here and there
With their small feet so cold and bare.

I caught a snowflake on my tongue, I wanted to see its size and shape
But when I opened, it was too late.

I shiver as the coldness reaches out for me,
I best get in before the heat leaves me.

The open fire glowing bright,
Looked like burning dragons and gave me a fright.

I hugged myself and sat tight,
Making sure it wouldn't bite.

I watched children's hair go from black to white,
The snow was like paint, changing everything in my sight.

Serena Sharma (11)
North Primary School, Southall

Seasons

Follow of the bird sound, feathers,
Leaves and stones all
Lead on to a new warm summer land,
The sun shines up with the brightness
This then will lead us to autumn
And unknown days to go
Trees tremble as you pass
Rise and fall of breath
Sign beneath your every step
Now the bird sound is gone
And you feel small and alone
Frightened wind grows cold
The autumn trees lose
Its leaves as the season turns
To winter
In winter fields are covered with snow
Then it's back to summer again
The sun shines down
The sun has lent its dying light to the land
Follow the flame
Follow the shadow
You dream of bird sounds and clouds
Feathers and branches full of leaves
To turn the shadow and the smell of earth
Enjoyable to see the greening spring's rebirth
Blossom like flowers in the spring of love
Or burn like a fire
Will we
Change with time
In the season of life.

Karsana Muhunthan (8)
North Primary School, Southall

My Family

I think my mum is bossy,
I think my mum is kind.
I think my mum is crazy,
But I don't really mind.

I think my dad is scary,
I think my dad is huge.
I think my dad is hairy,
But I am still confused.

I think my brother is bratty,
I think my brother is mad.
I think my brother is difficult,
But sometimes I am glad.

I think my grandpa is busy,
I think my grandpa is loud.
My granny always laughs at me,
Because my jokes make her proud.

Although I think all these things,
I know we have a laugh.
I can see us all smiling,
In a happy photograph.
Even though my family can be all of these things,
I know one thing for sure.
I love my family how they are
Because they all mean so much more.

Harsimrat Heer (7)
North Primary School, Southall

The Best Things About Football

Thierry Henry is the best
Ronaldinho is obsessed
Carlos hits the ball so hard
Kaka gave Rooney a birthday card!

Cafu is just like Nesta
Del Piero plays for Leicester
Tonight Inter play AC Milan
Unfortunately they've got a three match ban!

In the 1970s Maradona was skilful
In the middle of the match the referee got a call.

Pele scored loads of goals
In an advert Lampard played all the roles
Steven Gerrard plays his best
Oh, come on, give him a rest!

Football is my dream!

Samsher Dhami (10)
North Primary School, Southall

Arsenal

Football is great
Football is fantastic
Football is excellent
Football is exciting
Football is fun
Football is the best
Football is good
Football is enjoyable
Football is really, really fun and great.

Santa Chana (10)
North Primary School, Southall

Hideous Trolls And Mischievous Pixies

Under the bridge live hideous trolls
Their job, you may ask, is digging holes.
Scaring children is also what they do,
They even scare cows, the cows that go moo!
Big hairy giants scare humans away,
How they do it, I cannot say.
Everyday they eat fresh meat,
And, oh my, they aren't very neat!
A giant is a deadly dragon,
It gets transported in a little wagon!
Huge red dragons live in caves near mountains,
They drink from the finest hot fountains.
The ferocious things would breathe a fireball,
Oh, and one thing, they aren't very tall!
Green ugly ogres act like pigs,
All they eat is thin brown twigs!
They live in a tiny, lonely house,
And running on the floor is a little white mouse.

Optimistic fairies dancing in the air,
You wouldn't find a fairy in a funfair.
Fairies can have any name,
It could be tacky, it could be lame!
Pixies are mischievous things,
I don't know if a pixie sings.
Pixies help around the house,
Yet they could scare a little mouse!
Unicorns are pretty
You wouldn't find one in a city.
Some people say unicorns don't exist,
But you don't know they could be in the mist!

Amandeep Khera (9)
North Primary School, Southall

Monster Madness

Scary creatures lurk in the sky
You don't need to cry.
If I was you, in bed I would lie
Scary ghosts making shepherd's pie
Scary creatures lurk in the sky.

Witches and wizards in the sky
Wicked witches wanted children to cry
And they cry and cry
Witches crying as loud as blue whales whistles
Witches and wizards in the sky.

Gory griffins flying in the sky
Griffins are strange flying flies
But they have golden eyes
Don't believe the griffin lies!
They would leave you to your demise.

Terrible trolls have good noses
And they love to strike poses.
They can twist you into a roll
Mix you up in a cooking bowl.
Terrible trolls have good noses.

Happy light darted in the room
With a flash, bang, *boom!*
It was normal again.
Glad there are no more monsters.
Happiness joins us again
Are you up for a rhyming quest?

Devinder Chahal (10)
North Primary School, Southall

Magic Toys

Witches, wizards, magic toys,
Make the biggest noise.
People cry all the time,
Especially girls and boys.

The tall wizard has a long beard,
Ugly Mat, just never cared.
Some wizards are very small,
But can't hear your loud call!

Toys are faster than the lightning,
But they are rather frightening.
Toys win!
And witches sing?

Hooray for the toys,
And all the girls and boys.
Witches and wizards had to pay,
Children and toys win the day.

Hanish Panesar (10)
North Primary School, Southall

My Dogs

My dog is Chico,
Another is Patches.
They are so funny,
Hanging on when they chew,
Trying to bite all the time.

Bouncing football,
Jumping dogs.
Running and escaping,
Returning again.

Always fighting and
Biting each other.
Trying to go near them,
Watch them growling.

Don't touch him!
He's the moody one.
That's all I can tell you
My poem's done.

Brendan Gorman (9)
North Primary School, Southall

Horrible Witches

Bad witches came to town,
They turned the town right upside down.
They smelt of rotten cheese,
Made everyone eat mushy peas.
They ate mice and had head lice.

They turned the children into wizards
They turned the rest into lizards.
Wizards' tall hats reached the sky
One of the lizards told a big lie.
The fat wizards were so mean,
But the lizards started watching Mr Bean.

The witches' food was sickening
They read books by Charles Dickens.
The witches were world war soldiers
They only know how to be fighters.
The witches were mean, like a tyrant,
Witches are so mean.

The witches created magic toys
Some for girls and some for the boys.
The witches spell book ran across the room
The magic toys broke the witches' broom.
The witches tried to fix it
Instead, they bought a football kit.

The witches for the football fought,
Ended in hospital having a bad time.
Opportunists reign supreme
Wizards back to children,
Lizards are the rest
Happiness is just the best.

Paramvirpal Dhaliwal (10)
North Primary School, Southall

Wicked Beasts

Stinky ogres and trolls, they stink and have rolls
I saw they were ugly, I thought they were hungry
Beasts are fat, they eat bats, also stink like rats.
They sleep on dirty mats,
They never look clean,
Food on their clothes, show where it's been.
Beasts eat a lot in feasts; they eat a lot of meats.
They sleep like grisly bears
And their heads are shaped like pears.

Akash Mahay (10)
North Primary School, Southall

Fairy Poems

The bad wolf ran through
The forest like a motorbike
All he would do is run
Because he thought it was fun.

The ugly green ogre named Treck
Always loved a bath of mud.
He was a blissful green bean
The ugly green ogre is a mountain
That baths and has yellow teeth.

Ugly trolls have big moles
They are so smelly
They have no belly.
They live under bridges
So they go off their hinges.
Bliss chased the hideous trolls out from their caves and bridges
Now no more knocks, or fearful voices
Everyone can now rejoice.

Isaac Fazaldin (10)
North Primary School, Southall

Medieval Madness

The Grim Reaper, master of doom
Dragons' fire swoops across the room.
Deadly dragons, courageous knights,
Beasts, goblins have vicious fights.
Towering terrors, terrible trolls,
Ogres are such horrible spellers.

Gory griffins fly in the skies,
Woeful witches telling lies.
Beasts taking kids into cranberry pies!
Can't you feel the fear in your eyes?
Ghosts searching the Earth for hosts
Madmen eating turkey roast.

Serpents dwelling in the basements,
Ogres are like monkeys roaring in enjoyment.
Dragons and trolls have vicious fights
They both come over from the Northern Lights.
Giant bats eat rotten rats
Witches wear long pointy hats.

Bony beasts bashing bricks
Goblins play nasty tricks.
Knights are peacocks when they walk along bricks
Blood pouring down glass
Knights have fists of brass.

All of a sudden darkness leaves the room
A giant flash then a boom.
The villagers began to cheer
As the beasts flew away scared to the rear.

Arandeep Sidhu (9)
North Primary School, Southall

Respecting Our Planet

It's an amazing planet
Just like a cosy blanket.
Inside we're all the same
With different names.
Colourful, cheeky, caring cats.
But here comes the problem, *pollution!*
But we can't be so glum
What can we do?
We can't just say moo!
If the world's full of pollution - no more me or you!
There's not time to be sneaky or freaky.

To help, stop watching your cartoons
Clear up, the pollution will be gone soon.
Everybody can do something, just like lightning
We all respect each other
Just like your mother.
Remember everybody matters.
Pollution causes danger, but do not get anger
Collect it up and recycle.

If we try, we can make it stop
We must try to respect
Even if it's not perfect
It's an amazing planet
Just like a cosy blanket.

Vinthuya Ketheswaran (9)
North Primary School, Southall

Monkey

Monkeys are funny
They're cute like bunnies
Monkeys are light
They, of course fight.

Monkeys are silly
There's one named Billy,
Monkeys are stupid
They act like Cupid.

Monkeys are cute
The next minute they're mute.
Monkeys are crazy
Monkeys are not lazy.

They swing
They don't do bling.

Hamse Adam Mohamed (9)
North Primary School, Southall

Fairies

Fairies can fly in the sky
We all eat a big fat pie
When fairies sing
Then birds are merry
Fairies eat cherries
But never get merry.

Fairies can eat
But they have no beat.
Fairies on the wall
But they can't sing at all.
The fairies have a ball
But they can't call.

Fairies play with the mat
But they can't catch a cat.
Fairies get a treat
Then they eat some meat.
Fairies have a mouth
But they don't get loud.

Fairies are very light
They are also very bright.
All the fairies whizz in flight
They never have a fight.
Fairies are good
Like they know they should.

Ayesha Awan (10)
North Primary School, Southall

Vampire

Vampire, vampire, where are you?
Vampire, vampire, don't come out.
Vampire, vampire, you don't scare me.
You need fresh mints to cure that awful smell
And don't think about offering your rotten tea.
Stay in your coffin because I'm more boffin than you.
He wasn't scared of the cross,
He thought he was the boss.
I took a toss, he lost.
He hung me on the hook,
I said, 'What are you a cook?'
He sucked my blood, the fangs dug right into my skin
Whoosh, the cape went.
He returned to his coffin in Khartoum.

Kauthar Jama (10)
North Primary School, Southall

Hieroglyphics

The writing is on the wall.
The symbols say it all.
What do they mean?
Inside the pyramids they can be seen.

A language of pictures to make a sound.
Written also on papyrus and temples found.
The ancient Egyptians developed in the year 3100 BC
Painted on coffins as you can see.

With hieroglyphics you can spell your name
If you want, you can put it in a frame.
To find out how the Egyptians lived in the past.
You have to master the symbols fast.

Samera Iqbal (9)
North Primary School, Southall

The Unicorn

I am a unicorn
I live under a spell
I live in the forest
And on my neck hangs a bell.

I sleep under the tweeting birds
I eat by the weaving stream
Things are so lovely
I think it's a dream!

I gallop as I wait for
A rider to find me
Every day I think he's standing
Right behind me.

I wait for a loyal rider
Brave and strong
And if he isn't then
It's all going to be wrong.

He is handsome and rich
With a golden sword
He owns a castle
And is called a lord.

It happened one day
The rider came
He was handsome,
But, it started to rain.

He grabbed my saddle
And guided me out,
He showed me his castle
And the things about.

And we lived happily ever after
Everyone was full of joyful laughter.

Zeinab Al-Rekabi (10)
North Primary School, Southall

School

School is sometimes cool
And sometimes doesn't rule
I like the burning food
Which changes my mood.

I like playing catch
And seeing a match
I like running
But I hate seeing the London bombings.

I like art, last time I drew Bart
I like my primary school and I now think it's cool
I don't want to leave.

Moninder Sangha (11)
North Primary School, Southall

My Favourite Things

I like dogs
I like cats
One thing I hate is flying little bats.

They fly at night
Sleep all day
They look at the sights in the month of May.

I like rabbits
I like mice
One thing I hate is crawling little lice.

They are so small
They run and chase
They fall down because their trainers don't have a lace.

I like diamonds
The door goes *ding, ding*
There's a person with lots of *bling, bling!*

Tamara Beharry-Corbin (11)
North Primary School, Southall

When I Go To The Park

I wake up in the morning and it's really sunny
But my sister told me something very funny,
The next morning I went to the park
And when I came back it was really, really dark.
But there was something coming very, very soon
And that was the whitening moon.
I enjoyed my day trip to the park
But now it's getting really, really dark.

Sulu Haneefa (9)
North Primary School, Southall

Everyone Counts

In this world we're all the same,
The only difference is our names.
You might be rich and I might be poor,
But we're still humans and that settles all.
Just 'cause you think you've got wicked style
Don't brag about your cool, nonsense in your fact file.

If you can't hear or can't talk,
Have no arms or cannot walk,
You're still you and that's for sure.

Can't you see the suffering?
In this world people are dying,
Children in fear, heavily crying.
You're lucky, very lucky.
Don't take things for granted
Clean water, friends and family
Good education, what a sensation,
Of this beautiful human creation.

Give some money to charity
Just spare a penny for those in need.

Fathma Shabbir (10) & Shazia Shabbir (9)
North Primary School, Southall

Do You Know It's Christmas Time

Snow is falling,
Ice is building,
Snowman's creation,
In this celebration.

Children playing,
While carols are chanted,
Turkey roasting,
As trees planted.

Santa on his way
In his sleigh
Putting presents
And making people pleasant.

It's a time for everyone
To relax and have fun
It's a day to have peace and no crime
Do you know it's Christmas time?

Gerrard Jayaratnam (10)
North Primary School, Southall

It Is Christmas

It is Christmas
It is Christmas
It is Christmas again
Oh yes!

What shall we do?
First put up the decorations
Next decorate the Christmas tree!

What shall we do?
Why don't we make Turkish food for you and me?

Why don't we invite our cousins and friends?
Let's get our plates and cups
Let's have a fun party!

It is Christmas we're ready to celebrate, celebrate!

Harvin Dang (8)
North Primary School, Southall

Strange, Strange

Strange, strange is the little old man who lives in a grange.
Old, old, and they say he keeps a box full of gold.
Bowed, bowed is his thin little back which once was proud.
Soft, soft, are his steps as he climbs the stairs to the loft.
Black, black is the old shuttered house.
Does he sleep on a sack?
They say he does magic, that he can cast spells.
That he prowls round the garden listening for bells.
That he watches for strangers, hates every soul
And peers with his dark eyes through the keyhole.
I wonder, I wonder, as I lie in bed
He sleeps with his hat on his head.
Is he really a magician with an alter of stone or a lonely old gentleman
left alone.
I wonder, I wonder.

Meanuraj Navaneethan (9)
North Primary School, Southall

Pink

Pink that's shocking as loud as a shout.
Like a tropical fish with fins that furl and flare outrageously as wings.
Flamingo feathers, coral reefs, a swollen sun in a sea of cloud.
When all the sky is ablaze of pink.
Pink that starts raw as a prawn.

Najmah Jama (9)
North Primary School, Southall

The Scarecrow

The scarecrow in my garden
Gives me a fright
All the time it's scaring me
Morning and the night.

He tries to open the window
When the family's asleep
And when he manages to open it
It makes a loud creak!

I run to my mum and dad
And tell them to follow me
But when we get to the garden
The scarecrow's as stiff as a tree.

Joe Butterfield-Goard, Patrick Friel & Joe Ajudua (10)
Our Lady & St John's RC Primary School

World War II

It's not the First World War, it's the Second one.
And we're all sad that it has begun.
We don't know whether we'll win or lose
Everything has been rationed even clothes and shoes!

It started when Hitler annoyed England and France
So they both said, 'This is your last chance'
So they declared war on Germany
Hoping they would get victory.

The soldiers had a very big task
And everyone had their own gas mask.
Then after six whole years
Every single person hears.

It's the fifteenth of August and we've won the war!
But I can tell you, we don't want anymore.
Because an awful lot of people have got shot!

But as we remember back to when it begun
We also remember the moment we won
We're not happy because the war's just started.
We're all happy because the Germans have departed.

Cara Dickens (8)
Our Lady & St John's RC Primary School

Cats

Cats are soft and white,
They never ever bite,
They are lovely and cute
Cat's eyes glow in the dark,
And they really like going to the park.

Roshani Khokhar (7)
Our Lady & St John's RC Primary School

Autumn

The flowers have stopped growing,
They know it's time to die,
The leaves on the trees start falling
As the wind makes them fly.

It is the season of the fall,
Fires start their blazing,
As the sun decides
To stop its shining.

Ashes left from fires
From people down the street,
Celebrating about the fall
With everybody they meet.

Every single garden
Has smoke round it all!
They are joyfully celebrating
The season of the fall.

The smell of smoky bonfires
Is hanging in the air,
The fall has decided
To give the flowers no care!

The fire starts a-blazing
So keep your pets inside,
If you let them out
They'll have a big surprise.

Ellenor Breslin & Cara Dickens (8)
Our Lady & St John's RC Primary School

Sunset

Going through the day, 'til half-past three
When the sun's gazing down hills.
The sun's shrinking softly, slowly, shining,
Soaking into the ground.
As the sun's making progress going down,
It's making fire to crack glass.
Rippling reflections in the water and night begins to fall.

Joseph Cooper (8)
Our Lady & St John's RC Primary School

Flowers

Flowers are nice just like mice
They come in all different colours
Just like lovers
Flowers come in bags unlike tags.

They come in all sizes and shapes
Just like cakes
They look delicious
So I wonder if they're scrumptious.

Roses are red, violets are blue
So you must be too
I love the smell of flowers
Just like Alton Towers.

They are so right
Also really bright
They're the best thing ever
Unlike the weather.

Aaron Molloy (9)
Our Lady & St John's RC Primary School

Spring

Here comes the spring
Lots of things it brings.
Flowers popping through the ground
Lot of people all around.

Here comes the spring
The most helpful thing
Helps the farmers grow their crops
It really does help a lot.

Just enough rain, just enough sun
Just enough for everyone.

Rachel Da Cruz (9)
Our Lady & St John's RC Primary School

Food Fury

I saw a little mouse in his tiny house
His dinner was a woodlouse!
There was a rat who got eaten by a bat!
And that bat got eaten by a cat with a cool short hat.
Then the hat blew away, all the way to a waterfall
Then it fell to Hell!

Matthew Pereira (8)
Our Lady & St John's RC Primary School

Animals

Dogs, cats, fish and leopards, they're all animals.
They are cute forever and ever as I always say
They are always there to help me.
I love animals as I say
Because they're cute and always there.
And I am going to get one soon, so keep your feet steady here.

Zosia Suchcitz (8)
Our Lady & St John's RC Primary School

Summer

Here comes the summer, goodbye wind and rain
I can see the flowers through my windowpane.
All the grass is growing, all summer through
I see my mother putting on her shoe.

Look at all the trees growing in the sun
Me and my friends are all having fun.
I was playing on a rock
It got dark at eight o'clock.

Summer is the best, it beats all the rest.
It can't end, why does it end?

Leana Wise (9)
Our Lady & St John's RC Primary School

The Make A Poem Poem

I pick up a pen and paper and then I start to write and write
And when I get an idea I shout with delight.
I think about karate men who like to fight and fight
Magic beans, jelly witches and blue and green hinges.
Very ugly people cutting off their own hair
And a great gremlin's chair.
Little tiny and fat ants who like to scare.
Hairy cows and red towels and green wolves who don't howl.
Green magic gowns and an Eskimo's frown turn a nice
                                        chocolate brown.
Fires in little towns that make beeping sounds.
Baby dragons and silver hounds turn into green pound coins.
That's the end of the poem now make up your own!

Callum Bewick (8)
Our Lady & St John's RC Primary School

When I Grow Up

When I grow up I wanna get a horse
Because they look so lovely and have loads of force.

I will call her Fairy,
I will call him Harry,
I will call them any name,
Fame, Lame, Came.

When I grow up I wanna get a horse
Because they look so lovely and have loads of force.

I will call her Wigwam,
I will call him Traffic Jam,
I will call them any name,
Slam, Sham, Tram.

When I grow up I wanna get a cat
Because they look so scruffy and wear a hat.

I will call her Valley,
I will call him Alley,
I will call them any name,
Bawl, Crawl, Brawl.

Colleen McSweeney (8)
Our Lady & St John's RC Primary School

My Dog Called Dogger

I have a dog called Dogger
He is ever so fat but as small as a rat.
He's only a puppy but can be tough,
But when he wants a kiss, I say, 'Go away!'

Anyway, dog's sleep everywhere
On the sofa, on the chair, on the table, anywhere
They will even stay awake all night
But my little Dogger is the best; he just keeps on going on.

Shauna Mukhtar (9)
Our Lady & St John's RC Primary School

The Simpson Family

Don't call Homer fatty
Or he will hit you with Maggie.
Don't call Bart, brat
Or he will hit you with a bat.
Don't call Marge, rage
Or she won't give you a massage.
Don't call Lisa pizza
Or she will turn you into a freezer.

Reece Smith (8)
Our Lady & St John's RC Primary School

Greedy Dog

This dog will eat anything.
Apple cores and chicken fat,
Milk you poured out of a cat.
He likes the string that ties the roast,
And he likes to lick the coast.
Hide your chocolates! He's a thief,
He'll even lick the snot on your handkerchief!
If you have sudden shocks
Carefully conceal your socks.
Leave some soup without a lid
After that he'll eat your baby's bib.
When you think he's full up
You will find him gobbling bits of wool.
Orange peels or paper bags,
Dusters and old cleaning rags.
This dog will eat anything,
Except for mushrooms and cucumbers.
Now, what is wrong with those, I wonder?

Jessica Ajudua (8)
Our Lady & St John's RC Primary School

Food

Chocolate, dairy, some are hairy,
I love to eat you.
Burgers, chips, crisps and snacks
But if you eat too much
You might get a heart attack,
Or you might get fat!
So don't eat them a lot or you will want to stop.

Ice cream, biscuits, jelly beans sweets
These are a few of my favourite treats.
Stilton cheese, honey from bees, rotten eggs and fish,
These are the things that I think are rubbish.
So most food is great to eat but only for a treat,
But if you eat too much you will get fat.

James Gill (8)
Our Lady & St John's RC Primary School

Treasure Box

There is a treasure box in my room when I moved house.
There is a treasure box in my room and I am scared of opening it.
There might be a ghost, there might be a skeleton.
But whatever it is, I am not opening the treasure box.
I hide under the covers when I think of that treasure box.
It makes noises at night and opens and closes.
I am scared of the treasure box in my room.
My brother opened the treasure box and I screamed!
Inside the treasure box was a beautiful doll
And now I am not scared of the treasure box.

Shannon Friel (8)
Our Lady & St John's RC Primary School

Fred The Sleepyhead

I'm Fred; I sleep on my mum's bed,
But not when I'm being fed
You will find me on my mum's bed
So I'm Fred the sleepyhead.
I like my mum's red bed,
Sometimes I hate being fed and I love going to bed.
And don't wake up Fred the sleepyhead
You will get scratched if you wake me up.

Tyler De Guzman (8)
Our Lady & St John's RC Primary School

Juggler

Eyes on the equipment on the double,
But you might get into trouble.
You have to run because they want some tricks
But they see a person picks.

Animals in the fair.
Something like an elephant, sometimes like to scare
So the mayor comes out
And said, 'Do it correct, before I shout!'

Thomas Barreto (7)
Our Lady & St John's RC Primary School

Football

I'm feeling crazy, I'm football mad
Grab a ball and try and be the best player in the land.
Try and beat me, try and beat me
If you do not beat me you will have to treat me.
Now you have to treat me to a football match
And I hope my favourite football team does not end up in a
dusty patch.

Connor Hagerty (8)
Our Lady & St John's RC Primary School

Animals

Animals here, animals there
Animals flying in the air.

Animals far, animals near,
Animals climbing up the pier.

Animals dogs, animals cats,
Animals mice, animals bats.

Animals are butterflies flying in the air,
Animals are spiders, I hope people care.

Eimer O'Sullivan (8)
Our Lady & St John's RC Primary School

The Sky Diving Dame

Look, a sky diving dame
That's a shame
She's quite big, she might squash
She has done that, it's posh.

Daniel Cussons (8)
Our Lady & St John's RC Primary School

The Deep Sea Groove

If you're under the sea where the water's blue
And you see an octopus looking at you
Don't be scared, just say hello
Because under the sea music is mellow.

Booga, booga, booga, booga, deep sea groove
Booga, booga, booga, booga deep sea move.
That's the way to do the deep sea groove.

Up above the seagulls squawk
The dolphins leap and the parrots talk.
They squeak and shriek and natter and chatter
Cos under the sea music matters.

Hannah McGovern (8)
Our Lady & St John's RC Primary School

I Know An Old Lady

I know an old lady that swallowed a bat,
That's why she is big and fat.
I know an old lady that swallowed a spoon,
It went ting, tang and bang
And that's how she got so fat, lick a bat.

Thomas Gilbert (8)
Our Lady & St John's RC Primary School

Animals

I have a horse
And he is on the right course
I have a parrot
And he is like a giant carrot.
I have a monkey
That likes to be funky.
I have a dog
That likes the log.
I have a . . .

Holly Serrao (8)
Our Lady & St John's RC Primary School

What Is Yellow?

Yellow is the shining sun
Yellow is a big banana
Yellow is a shooting star
Yellow is a bumblebee.

Chris Domingues Vallely (7)
Our Lady & St John's RC Primary School

Which One Are You?

Look at me
Look at him
Just the same
Just my twin
We're both fair
We've got the same hair
We've got the same coats
We've got the same boats
Our names are Rashel and Lashel.

Ana Rita Da Costa Mota (8)
Our Lady & St John's RC Primary School

Friends

I have a friend named Connor,
He always gives me the honour.
We like to play with bits and bobs
And to be a friend of Connor is an honour.

I have a friend named Hill
He went to pay my bill,
We like to run up and down
And never pay my bill.

I have a friend named Amy
She fancies my brother Jamie
We like to play pat-a-cake
And please bake me a cake.

Alessandro Salomon (8)
Our Lady & St John's RC Primary School

The Body

We are the body
Pigs are dummies.

We bodies are clever
Bodies have a liver.

Hearts keeps us alive
My heart's just arrived.

Brains keeps us clever
Shoes are made out of leather.

The body has eyes
We've got lives.

Bodies have bones
So do camels.

Hill Denny (8)
Our Lady & St John's RC Primary School

Silly People

Hannah is a spanner
Alanna is a banana
Holly is a lolly
Amy loves Jamie
Michael is a bicycle
Hill is a hill
Sam loves ham
Deborah is a zebra
And Amy loves Jamie.

Amy Kemp (7)
Our Lady & St John's RC Primary School

On The Roller Coaster

Once on the roller coaster
Way up high,
A shiny gold dove
Waiting to fly.

Once on the roller coaster
Not holding onto the bars,
Very small things
Looking like cars.

Once on the roller coaster
Here and again,
People not on the roller coaster
Still counting to ten.

Kiera Beirne (7)
Our Lady & St John's RC Primary School

God

God, God, He's as good as gold
God, God, He's never bold.
God, God, He is so sweet
God, God, He deserves a treat.
God, God, He is so cool,
God, God, He is not a fool.

God, God, He always loves,
God, God, He is like a dove.
God, God, He gives loads of hugs,
God, God, He even treats thugs.
God, God, He really likes a rhyme,
God, God, He loves lemon and lime.

God, God, He never lies,
God, God, He loves pies.
God, God, He doesn't die,
God, God, He has a big thigh.
God, God, He loves Elvis Presley
God, God, He loves the name Lesley.
God, God, God,
God, *be good.*

Sam Magee (8)
Our Lady & St John's RC Primary School

Please Ms Grimshaw

(Based on 'Please Mrs Butler' by Allan Ahlberg)

'Please Ms Grimshaw
This boy Dominic Sims
Keeps talking to me Ms
What shall I do?'

'Hide yourself in the cupboard, dear
Run away to sea
Take yourself to the roof, my lamb
Do whatever you think.'

'Please Ms Grimshaw
This boy Dominic Sims
Keeps taking my rubber Ms
What shall I do?'

'Hide it under your vest dear
Throw it in the sink
Swallow it if you like
But don't ask me!'

Alex Yeghiazarian (8)
Our Lady & St John's RC Primary School

What The Giant Ate For Dinner

First
He ate bees.

Next
He ate
Some chestnut trees.

Then
He ate
A house near me.

Last
Of all
He drank the sea.

Deborah Shoroye (7)
Our Lady & St John's RC Primary School

In The World . . .

In the world you get
Smelly socks and very hard rocks.
In the world you get
Stinky cheese and people saying please.
In the world you get
Tall boys and small boys.
In the world you get
A cat swallowing up a mat.
In the world you get
A man with a tan.
In the world you get
A car which can go really far.
In the world you get
A pet with a vet.
In the world you get
A woman called Pat with a brown mat.

George Stow (8)
Our Lady & St John's RC Primary School

Up, Up And Away

Up, up and away I'm in the sky
I can see people running by.
The grass is green, the sky is blue
I'm flying round, up and down.
Spinning mad, I feel so glad.
If this flight ends, I'll run to my friends
I'm sorry to say it is the end of my day,
See you later.

Jack Tilling (9)
Our Lady & St John's RC Primary School

Our World

Imagine yourself in a wonderful world
A place where normal is weird
Their world is straight, where our world is curled
And a bicycle cannot be steered.

People are rare and spiders are in abundance
Nobody wants to wear some clothes
Everybody loves to jump and prance
But nobody ever loathes
You think this place is crazy, when this world is yours.

Thomas Sylvester (10)
Our Lady & St John's RC Primary School

Friends Poem

Friends, everybody loves friends
Friends are there for friends,
They are everywhere.
Wherever you go, whatever you do,
Friends are always there.
For what you do they will always be there,
If you are hurt, friends are always there.
My friend, my friend is called Phoebe,
In every way she's very funny.
I really like my best friend,
Friends are loving and caring,
That is my best friend.

Eleanor Thompson (9)
Our Lady & St John's RC Primary School

Wonderful Seasons!

Autumn leaves fall from the trees
Then they are swept away with a big breeze.
Winter snow falls from the sky,
The coldness could almost make you die.
Spring, all the birds sing and the trees bloom
It is such a happy season, there is no gloom!
Summer, people lie on the golden sand on the beach
In their bikinis that are peach.

Rebecca Fegan (10)
Our Lady & St John's RC Primary School

A Riddle Of Secrets

It will keep your secrets in place
And no one will take it away
If someone tries to snatch it
They'll have a riot catching it.

Maegan Alexander (10)
Our Lady & St John's RC Primary School

I Want To . . .

I want to paint the scent of a purple flower.
I want to touch the sound of a robin's voice
in the snow-covered garden.
I want to taste the time slowly pass by,
I want to see the exact second when a flower dies
and falls to the cold ground.
I want to taste the heat of the sun on a hot summer's day.
I want to use all of my senses hearing, sight, taste, smell and touch.

Daniel Branston (10)
Our Lady & St John's RC Primary School

Autumn

Autumn is a time when the leaves fall off the trees
And they all get very crusty like bread rolls.
But when the sun and rain come out,
The leaves will grow again.
So watch out for more leaves
Because they might get in your way.

Sascha Aurora-Lei Choy (10)
Our Lady & St John's RC Primary School

Summer

Summer, summer
You're so bright.
Summer, summer
You are so great.
Summer, summer
You are so hot.
Summer, summer
You are so nice.
Summer, summer
Do come back.

Hannah Lenkiewicz (10)
Our Lady & St John's RC Primary School

Travelling Round The World

I've travelled the world countries one by one,
Every country is great fun.
Rich, poor, famous, polite
It's so nice, it's such a delight.
Now it's time for me to go
Sun, rain and also snow.

Christiana Pires (9)
Our Lady & St John's RC Primary School

The Little Trumpet

There once was a trumpet lying in the shop
waiting to be bought not for a lot
One day the shopkeeper said, 'You must be alone, I'll look after you'
'Thank you,' the little trumpet said,
now he's happy because they're famous.

Gregory Lipka (9)
Our Lady & St John's RC Primary School

Zoo Animals

When you go to this zoo there are a few things you must know . . .
When you go to the elephants, this is what you may spy
A crazy little elephant called Kly Kly!
If you dare go to the monkey cage
Beware! Watch out!
For there's a cheeky little monkey who will nip your hat
So watch out for that!
And finally if you visit the penguins
They will show off and swim.
But the best one of all is called Kim.
Oh yes, before you leave make sure you have not fed any of them
They might go a bit hyper.

Hayley Gilbert (9)
Our Lady & St John's RC Primary School

Christmas Pud

I love the smell of carrots
Soaking in the pan,
I love the smell of Brussels sprouts
Straight out of the can.
I love the taste of ham
Pink and juicy too,
I love the taste of roasted spuds
That are a golden hue.
I love my chewy Christmas dinner
But the thing I like the best
Is the fiery Christmas pudding
If there's any left!

Aisling McConville (9)
Our Lady & St John's RC Primary School

Who Am I?

My first is in sun but not in fun
My second is in cat but not in hat
My third is in Hannah but not in Anna
My fourth is in coat and also in oat
The next is in octopus with eight legs in the sea
My last is in lasagne and I'm having it for tea!
What am I?

Hannah Burke (9)
Our Lady & St John's RC Primary School

My Dog

My dog is called Barney
He is a Labrador
And he sleeps on the floor.
On his hind legs, he'll struggle to open the door
Or he'll wiggle his nose and tickle his paws.
He dreams in his sleep and often snores.
While he is sleeping, he'll whimper and whine
You'd never believe he was having a good time.
But one thing's for certain, we should be allowed
To stop dear old Barney when he starts snoring!

Amy Hodges (10)
Our Lady & St John's RC Primary School

Animals

A cute little kitten to cuddle up to,
A sweet little puppy that is so lucky,
A fluffy little rabbit that hopes here and there,
And a strange little guinea pig with lots of hair
A tiny hamster running on its wheel
And a cute little goldfish swimming here and there.

Rebecca O'Sullivan (10)
Our Lady & St John's RC Primary School

Bright Different Colours

There are all different colours
That all look nice and bright
And all of the different colours are used like stars at night.
But when it starts to rain, rain, rain
It makes the lovely rainbows bright.
And out comes the sun
That dries up all the rain.
When everybody's playing the colours just appear
But when everybody's inside asleep
There's no colour out at all.

Phoebe Rodrigues Ejegi (9)
Our Lady & St John's RC Primary School

The Girl I Know

The girl I know doesn't speak,
The girl I know can't play hide-and-seek,
The girl I know does not dare move out of turn,
The girl I know loves black,
The girl I know loves following me everywhere,
The girl I know has the same features as me,
The girl I know is my shadow.

Imogen Young (10)
Our Lady & St John's RC Primary School

Dragons

Demon eyes grab your breath,
No matter where you hide
They're there watching you, watching you.

Flames frying you the second it touches your skin,
In the wind you hear the wings,
Which have enough energy to blow you away.

Don't know which way to turn
For their sharp claws imprison you
You shout and scream but no one can hear.

You try to escape but the razor-sharp teeth pick you up by the shirt
You try running in the air, though you get nowhere
No matter how fast you run.

Tara Burrell (10)
Our Lady & St John's RC Primary School

Bill's Nightmare

The bell has gone
The kids come out
There are tons of children running about
Behind the bushes
Keeping still
There's a horrible creature
Waiting for Bill!
Bill walks out
The creature follows
Bill goes home to see his cat Mellor
But the disgusting creature decides to come
Up in his room where Bill feels warm
All of his skin gets torn
His bones smash
And break to pieces
The creature has to dash
It's another day
And the kids start to play
But the creature is there again!

Rebecca Slack (10)
Our Lady & St John's RC Primary School

The Troll, The Troll

The troll, the troll
Who had a big mole
Went on the pitch
To eat up the kicks
But accidentally scored a great goal
By kicking off his mole
But he upset the kids
Playing like Ryan Giggs!

Conor Molyneaux (10)
Our Lady & St John's RC Primary School

The Story Of Love

Roses are red
Violets are blue
My heart is broken
Your loving tender kiss
Haunts me in the night
Your loving tender hair
Soft and silky shine
And you blossomed
In my eyes.

Patrick Harvey (10)
Our Lady & St John's RC Primary School

Dragons

The demon eyes looking at you
Blowing his flaming breath directly through
Flapping its wings and moving along
Looking for more towns to burn so strong.
When will it end?
When will it be?
Think abut a century to see!

Christian Sahakian (11)
Our Lady & St John's RC Primary School

Amazement

Amazement is turquoise emerald.
It tastes like myself.
It smells like a helpless bat.
It looks like a tiger.
It sounds like a loud scream.
It feels like a dog's sticky tongue.

Jack Richards (7)
SS Mary & Peter CE Primary School, Teddington

Happiness

Happiness is yellow like a golden ring.
It tastes like silky lemonade.
It smells like melted chocolate.
It looks like a golden star.
It sounds like a drop of rain in a river.
It feels like a butterfly flying.

Alice Stapleton (8)
SS Mary & Peter CE Primary School, Teddington

Love

Love is crimson like a dark red love heart.
It tastes like sweet, sweet honey.
It smells like sweet red roses.
It looks like sunlight.
It sounds like a beautiful sound.
It feels like a lovely birthday cake.

Emily Wotton (7)
SS Mary & Peter CE Primary School, Teddington

Fear

It is crimson-red.
It tastes disgusting.
It sounds like a bang.
It feels like a creepy crawling on you.
It smells like a poisonous flower.
It looks like a full ice-cold moon.

Jack Fifield (8)
SS Mary & Peter CE Primary School, Teddington

Amazement

Amazement is yellow like the sun.
It tastes like candyfloss.
It smells like caramel.
It looks like a child who's just discovered the world is made of chocolate.
It sounds like a merry-go-round.
It feels like melted toffee.

William Stewart (7)
SS Mary & Peter CE Primary School, Teddington

Amazement

Amazement is yellow like a burning sun.
It tastes like a new bar of chocolate.
It smells like a new present.
It looks like the whizz of a magic wand.
It sounds like a quiet day.
It feels great!

Grace Kelly (7)
SS Mary & Peter CE Primary School, Teddington

Happy

Happy is yellow like the sun.
It tastes like cake.
It smells like the best roses.
It looks like a smile.
It sounds like a laugh.
It feels like the softest velvet.

Rosie Hurley (8)
SS Mary & Peter CE Primary School, Teddington

Sad

Sad is the colour black like a bin's shadow.
It tastes like a poison bite.
It smells like rotten eggs.
It looks like everyone else is happy.
It sounds like boom.
It feels like gloom.
Oh, what a bad thing it is.

Cameron Hughes (8)
SS Mary & Peter CE Primary School, Teddington

Shock

Shock makes you want to cry.
It is silver.
It tastes like orange.
It smells like smoke in the cold sky.
It looks like thunder crashing through the sky.
It sounds like rain dropping down onto the ground.
It feels like electricity whizzing through you.

James Gawn (7)
SS Mary & Peter CE Primary School, Teddington

Happiness

Happiness is yellow like the sun.
It tastes like sweets.
It smells like chocolate.
It looks like the sea.
It sounds like people cheering.
It feels like swimming in the sea.

Jasmine Belaid (7)
SS Mary & Peter CE Primary School, Teddington

Love

Love is the colour of purple.
It tastes sweet and strong.
It smells like roses.
It sounds like people kissing.
It feels like having a marriage.

James Ruddick (7)
SS Mary & Peter CE Primary School, Teddington

Happiness

Happiness is yellow like a sun shining on a gloriously sunny day.
It tastes like rich brown chocolate.
It smells like the sweet scent of daffodils.
It looks like a rainbow upon the sea.
It sounds like busy bees in the countryside.
It feels like someone cuddling me.

Jane Li (8)
SS Mary & Peter CE Primary School, Teddington

Shock

Shock is like a white flash.
It tastes like cold snow.
It smells like venom from a snake.
It looks completely colourless.
It sounds like someone screaming.
It feels like splinters.

Edward Ross (8)
SS Mary & Peter CE Primary School, Teddington

Happiness

Happiness is yellow like the sun shining.
It tastes like chocolate melting in your mouth.
It smells like sweet sugar.
It looks like a pile of gold.
It sounds like the tinkling of the piano.
It feels like you have just won the lottery!

Lucy Good (8)
SS Mary & Peter CE Primary School, Teddington

Amazed

Amazed is the colour of gold.
It smells like ice cream and sweets.
It looks like sugar and chocolate.
It tastes like bang and boom, whizz and pop!
It sounds like crash or thunder, pop, bang, boom!
It feels like whizz, fizz, bang, boom!

Francesca Edmonds (7)
SS Mary & Peter CE Primary School, Teddington

Sad

Sad is black like a dark cave.
It tastes like rotten eggs.
It smells like smoke pouring out of a chimney.
It looks like teardrops pouring out of somebody's eyes.
It sounds like somebody screaming.
It feels like running water.

Rhys Stratton (8)
SS Mary & Peter CE Primary School, Teddington

Christmas

Christmas is bright,
The baubles are light,
There's lots of ice,
And I think that's nice,
I love Christmas because it's fun.

Christmas is flash,
But there is no cash,
All the presents are mine,
And I think that's fine,
I love Christmas because it's fun.

Sam Hill (11)
SS Mary & Peter CE Primary School, Teddington

I Wonder What The Moon Thinks?

I wonder what the moon thinks.
He probably thinks I'm strange,
Staring up at him from the Earth
From a very long, long range.

I wonder what the moon does
Is he friends with all the stars?
Maybe he phones Jupiter
And plays cards with Mars.

I wonder how the moon feels
When he's ill who checks his health?
Maybe I'll build a rocket one day
And ask him that myself.

Grace Ruddick (11)
SS Mary & Peter CE Primary School, Teddington

Loneliness

Loneliness is black like the dark, mad, hazy, mazy cave.
It tastes like bitter, bitter sea.
It smells like celery.
It looks like a tall troll.
It sounds like lightning.
It feels like being dead.

Sunny Curtis (8)
SS Mary & Peter CE Primary School, Teddington

Snowflakes

Every winter the snowflakes fall
Glittering like a little star
And as they fall they shine so brightly
Shining in the winter sun.
And yet everyone is different
In its own lovely way.
Everyone has a special pattern
That too is lovely for just one second.
But did you know, that no designer could match the patterns
on the snowflake?
Like tiny ice stars they fall, landing down upon the ground.
The snowflakes stop falling and start to settle,
A white blanket over the Earth.

Becky Cooke (10)
SS Mary & Peter CE Primary School, Teddington

Happiness

The colour of happiness is blue
Like the pale blue sky.
It tastes like sweet, soft and sugary lemonade.
The smell is as lovely as lavender.
It looks fun and full of merry music.
The sound is like running river.
It feels like a pleasant walk.

Harmony Leung (7)
SS Mary & Peter CE Primary School, Teddington

Loneliness

Loneliness is white like nothing.
Loneliness tastes like boiled rice.
Loneliness smells like bitter cold wind.
Loneliness looks like a dove flying.
Loneliness sounds like a smooth thing.
Loneliness feels like an empty room.

Georgia Jay (7)
SS Mary & Peter CE Primary School, Teddington

Anger

Anger is like dark danger.
Anger tastes like a bitter onion.
Anger smells like smoke from the oven.
Anger looks like a flash of lightning.
Anger sounds like a scared screech.
Anger feels like drizzling rain.

Alec Thomson (7)
SS Mary & Peter CE Primary School, Teddington

Happiness

Happiness is as yellow as a shooting star.
It tastes like hot chocolate and as smooth as a smoothie.
It smells like a million super-scented roses that's as scented as rosemary.
It looks like a heart that is as red as bright blood.
It sounds like whizzing fireworks that's as fast as light.
It feels like a soft doll and as soft as a pillow.

Dylan Rubini (8)
SS Mary & Peter CE Primary School, Teddington

Embarrassment

The colour of embarrassment is red like a daredevil.
It tastes like the salty seas.
It smells like clean clothes.
It looks like shallow seas.
It sounds like a crashing cave.
It feels like a hot dashing day.

Jack Williams (7)
SS Mary & Peter CE Primary School, Teddington

Anger

Anger is as red as a flickering flame.
It tastes like a scorched apple.
It smells like a devil that hasn't washed in days.
It looks like a red flaming rocket.
It sounds like a crashing car.
It feels like a fury arrow.

Mark Sandford (8)
SS Mary & Peter CE Primary School, Teddington

Love

Love is pink like a new blossomed petal.
Love tastes like a warm Christmas pudding.
Love smells like a fresh-blown kiss.
Love looks like a baby's first smile.
Love sounds like a newborn chick.
Love feels like a mother's first sight of her baby.

Margot Blackman (7)
SS Mary & Peter CE Primary School, Teddington

Anger

Anger's black like stormy sky.
It tastes like cold grey porridge.
It smells like soggy wet dogs.
It looks like a damp spooky house.
It sounds like a blazing tornado.
It feels like a prick of a needle.

Amelia Coyne (7)
SS Mary & Peter CE Primary School, Teddington

Hate

Hate is black like a stormy sky.
It tastes like cold muddy water.
It smells of cold pasta.
It looks like the devil's face.
It sounds like stabbing daggers.
It feels like your best friend is your worst enemy.

Alfie Jackson (8)
SS Mary & Peter CE Primary School, Teddington

Love

Love is red like a rose.
Love tastes like a cherry.
Love smells like a box of chocolates.
Love looks like a starry sky.
Love sounds like a bird singing.
Love feels like my first hug.

Mir Mason-Smith (8)
SS Mary & Peter CE Primary School, Teddington

Love

Love is red like a rose.
Love tastes like a bit of chocolate cake.
It smells like the scent of a rose.
It looks like the bride's dress.
Love sounds like a love song.
Love feels like a petal of a flower.

Brigitte Stander (7)
SS Mary & Peter CE Primary School, Teddington

Fun

Fun is red, pink and blue like a rainbow.
Fun tastes like sweets.
Fun smells like the sun.
Fun looks like friends.
Fun sounds like fun.
Fun feels like happiness.

Lucy Green (8)
SS Mary & Peter CE Primary School, Teddington

Sadness

Sadness is blue like the colour of the sky.
Sadness tastes like salt.
It smells like the air on a snowy day.
It looks like someone is alone.
It sounds like when someone is crying.

Joanna Rhys-Maitland (8)
SS Mary & Peter CE Primary School, Teddington

Love

Love is pink as a rose.
It tastes like a chocolate cake.
It smells like a jasmine in spring.
It looks like a soft bear.
It sounds like a sweet hummingbird.
It feels like a nice picnic.

Katie Hill (8)
SS Mary & Peter CE Primary School, Teddington

Fun

Fun is like eating a chocolate bun.
Colour of the blazing sun.
It smells as sweet as ice cream.
It looks like your friend playing with you.
It sounds as fun as a bouncy castle.
It feels like the best thing on Earth.

Luke Lanigan (7)
SS Mary & Peter CE Primary School, Teddington

Hate

Hate is red like the blood of a devil.
Hate tastes like raw carrots with jam.
Hate reeks of rotten cauliflower.
Hate looks like a ball of flame.
Hate sounds like thunder and lightning.
Hate feels like a devil destroying you.

Gavin Sandford (8)
SS Mary & Peter CE Primary School, Teddington

Love

Love is a beautiful rose.
Love tastes of strawberry.
It smells of something drifting from a kitchen.
It looks like hearts.
Love sounds like a heartbeat.
Love feels gentle.

Evangelina Perdoni (7)
SS Mary & Peter CE Primary School, Teddington

Love

Love is like a pink dreamy cloud.
It tastes like candyfloss on a stick.
It smells like a box of chocolates.
It likes a starry night.
It sounds like the sea.
It feels like a warm bed.

Clodagh Green (7)
SS Mary & Peter CE Primary School, Teddington

Fun

Fun is red like a clown's nose.
It tastes like lots of sweets.
It smells like fizzy pop.
It looks like a green day in the playground.
It sounds like screaming and shouting children.
It feels like me holding onto the side of the slide.

Isobel Chant (7)
SS Mary & Peter CE Primary School, Teddington

Happiness

Happiness is yellow like the boiling hot sun.
It tastes like warm custard pie.
Happiness smells like curry and rice.
It looks like sparkling light.
Happiness sounds like fun and laughter.
It feels like everyone's together.

Elliott Poley (7)
SS Mary & Peter CE Primary School, Teddington

Happiness

Happiness is green like grass in a field.
Happiness tastes like ice lollies.
Happiness smells like hot chocolate.
Happiness looks like a hug.
Happiness sounds like laughing children.
Happiness feels like my friends.

Morgan Skinner (7)
SS Mary & Peter CE Primary School, Teddington

Hate

Hate is as red as fire.
It tastes like chilli.
It smells like smoke.
It looks like a ball of fire.
It sounds like a storm.
It feels like burning alive.

Oliver Wood (8)
SS Mary & Peter CE Primary School, Teddington

Lonely

Lonely is black like the dark night sky.
It tastes like gruel in cold ice weather.
It smells like burnt porridge in steamy hot fire.
It looks like a black damp tyre in hot steamy sun.
It sounds like an echo of tears streaming in a river.
It feels like a person locked in a room.

Isabella Wateridge (8)
SS Mary & Peter CE Primary School, Teddington